A Profitable Love Affair

How to Build and Sustain A Strong Brand

Fiona Johnson-Davis

ISBN: 978-1-928155-91-1

PUBLISHED BY:
10-10-10 PUBLISHING
MARKHAM, ON
CANADA

Contents

Thank you to Emily and Lewis,
my beautiful daughter and gorgeous son,
David, my supportive and loving husband,
his lovely children, Antonia and Hugo,
my Dad Eric, who at 91 is an inspiration
and to all my friends, who have supported me.

Foreword

Over the course of a business's lifetime, it may flounder a bit and run off-course as it finds itself pulled and tugged in different directions. Fiona Johnson-Davis has a passion for helping a business get back on course and find its proper direction; she calls this 'rediscovering the mojo'.

Fiona's story is a fascinating one; what is most engaging to me is how she has used her life experiences, personal and professional, to help others see how they can affect their own experiences, both personally and professionally. When I first met Fiona I was struck by her compassion for others. She balances vision with pragmatism, and creativity with practicality, to create a vision for success in everyday commercial life. She is a creative spirit who truly connects with people on a personal level. She has affection for the business owner and knows how to use her skills to help these businesses discover what they want to be.

In A Profitable Love Affair, Fiona's passion is to help businesses determine why they exist, what they represent to their customers, and how they can deliver a 'wow' experience day in, day out. She shares her experience in building a brand and in translating the world of brands in straightforward language. She demonstrates what it takes to build a successful customer proposition into a successful business.

Fiona's empathy for others, combined with her strength of belief, her insight, and her energy, enable her to guide her clients to make great business decisions. If you are a business owner or in a leading role in a business that requires fresh thinking and a step change in performance, this book's for you. I recommend you read Fiona's book and get in touch soon! www.thebrandinspirationco.com.

Raymond Aaron,
New York Times Top Ten Best-Selling Author

Testimonials

A Profitable Love Affair is part CV and business card, part autobiographical but most importantly a brand building masterclass. Fiona articulates a wealth of compelling insights that will enable any brand to connect better with their customers as well as evolve with them. Fiona's passion for supporting businesses to (re)discover their mojo is infectious. As a senior retail operations specialist with international experience there're many ideas that I would seek to incorporate in my own and colleagues practises.

Celine O'Connor Head of Central Operations, Blue Inc

At last! The intellect and warmth of character that Fiona Johnson-Davis demonstrates on a daily basis has finally been captured and written down for the benefit of others. That is what makes Fiona successful, her love and compassion for others who are making their way through their business journeys.

This book highlights some of the key struggles that Fiona faced and allows readers to feel safe in the knowledge that we aren't alone. She goes on to raise questions that prompt the reader to assess their own business, and how different approaches both mentally and practically can make a big difference to success.

Having seen Fiona in action giving sound advice to fledging business owners, I would encourage anyone to pick up a copy of *A Profitable Love Affair.*

Sophie Shrubsole - Head of Corporate Relations & Mentoring, Westminster Business Council

Women in Retail is a living testimony to the breadth and depth of Fiona's ability to define the absolute essence of a brand and ensure the full spirit is captured, understood and conveyed putting our community at the very heart of everything that we say and do. This book provides insight through the eyes and experiences of an instinctive customer expert who really has been there and done it - and still is! Her observations, explorations and experiences shared will ensure any business leader reading this book can transfer the learning into tangible benefits for their business.

Karen Richards - Founder & Director - Women in Retail

Having had many conversations with Fiona Johnson-Davis about business and brands I am so pleased that she has shared some of her stories and insights in this book. She is pragmatic and insightful and has a way of making clear and real a concept - branding - that can be hard to pin down.

Sally Bibb, Founder of Engaging Minds and author

Introduction
Who? What? Where? Why?

Who are your customers? What role does your brand play in the lives of your customers? Where will your brand be in the future? What will it take to ensure that the relationship between your brand and your customers will remain strong? Why does your brand exist? What are the consequences of not being able to answer these questions about your business with confidence? Stick with me and I will explain why you should care about the answers to these questions. My story will address the parallels between developing and maintaining great personal relationships and building a strong brand for a successful business. It all comes down to relationships between people. Have you ever thought of it this way?

After reading this book you will know what it takes to not only create a strong brand, but also avoid losing touch with your customers' changing needs. I will (re)ignite your mojo – the 'Why', the 'What' and the 'How'! I will discuss ways you can discover the brand essence, the 'Why', that connects you with your customers.

Discovering the brand essence will make your business, product or service an integral part of the lives of your customers. Once you successfully convey your brand, your whole organisation and your customers will be captivated. When your brand values and beliefs are authentic and shared by you, your colleagues and stakeholders, your team act as a single, motivated, inspired team on behalf of your brand. If your people are 'living the brand' in all that they do to deliver your product or service, which is the 'What', they and their work will persuade your customers with ease.

It is not enough to come up with a great brand concept. To convince your customers, your brand essence must inform and be reflected in everything you do. This is the 'How' and it must be extraordinary and consistent. I believe that the brand is the business and the business is the brand; for success, the two must be one and the same. Included in your business and brand are the product, its price, your people, your service, the selling environment, that bit of extra-special something you might never have thought of or dared to try on your own. When your mojo is (re)ignited you will deliver on the brand promise and delight your customers, day in and day out!

In Chapter 1 ("Why Should You Care?") we explore my beliefs and I set out why it will be worth your while reading on.

In Chapter 2 ("Some of the Great Love Affairs") we explore examples of some of the great brand growth stories. In Chapter 3 ("How fast Can You Fall (out of Love)?") we learn how quickly a brand can fall from favour. In Chapters 4-6 ("The Heart of the Matter") we learn how great product, customers who love you and colleagues who care are vital ingredients. Finally, in Chapter 7 ("Creating your own Love Affair") we will explore how to create your own successful brand.

I've based this book on my beliefs and hope that, at least to some extent, you will see the world from my perspective. I don't expect you to take my principles on trust; I promise that I'll share my evidence. I trust you'll enjoy our love affair!

Chapter 1
Why Should You Care?

My beliefs have been built over the course of my life and career, and they fundamentally influence my values, behaviour and the choices I make in life and work. I tend to be at my best when I balance my head and my heart, the practical and the intuitive. The yin and yang of seemingly contrary forces are actually complimentary. The whole is greater than the individual parts.

I remind myself not to be held back by the nagging doubt of 'what if', rather to be inspired by the opportunity to continue to learn by stepping outside of my comfort zone and acquiring new skills while living life to the full. I find confidence in understanding the context of a situation. For instance, having found maths tricky at school, it all fell into place when I needed to balance a till in time to catch the train home in my first job as a Management Trainee at Harvey Nichols!

Additionally, without being a natural linguist I achieved a good working proficiency in French within three weeks when, at age thirteen, I went on a French exchange to stay with a lovely and welcoming family just outside Paris. In both situations context was key!

Above all else, I value the people in my life. Secondly, I value my friendships and, thirdly, my career. To me it is fundamental to invest in relationships with the people I love, care for, trust and respect. My personal inspiration comes from the confidence resulting from having meaningful, empathetic and authentic relationships at home, at work and with friends. My greatest achievements are not career based; they are my children, Emily and Lewis, who are wonderful young adults and I am very proud of them both. I am also honoured to have two beautiful stepchildren, Antonia and Hugo, as I recently married my best friend, David. Our love affair is quite a story; stick with me and I'll share more once we get to know each other better.

Like many people I've had a few personal and professional battles along with barriers to overcome; but, overall, I wouldn't change a thing. The highs have been tremendous and the lows have taught me so much. Also, the highs have outweighed the lows by a long, long way…

I have not followed a career plan; rather I have remained open-minded to opportunities, as they have arisen. I've followed my instincts about what has felt right at each stage when I've had a choice to make. I've always followed my principles, which are to add real value, work with people I respect and trust, and feel a sense of fulfilment with whatever I'm doing.

Once I worked out and understood the context I found myself in, this gave me an enormous sense of security. Once I had that, confidence started to flow, allowing my intuitive side to come to the fore. This confidence to go my own way is not always with the full understanding of parents, my older sister, or husbands and boyfriends. But it has served me in good stead at crucial times of my career and life. Knowing when to move on, rather than be moved on, by grasping what's happening around me and then doing something about it has served me well. A characteristic that extends to my personal life as well as my business life. Once my mind is made up, I will quickly crack on to the next stage of life!

This has been a life that has not been without many battles and barriers to overcome. Being seen as the blonde, pretty one, rather than the brainy one, coupled with a career where the journey was much less clear than that of the 'professional' older sister was challenging. I managed to succeed in the earlier part of my career in a largely male world. However, I had to constantly prove myself and was on a path where being pregnant at the 'wrong time' could have been career limiting.

Failing the 11 plus; kicking teenage anorexia once big sister scared me into tackling it; struggling with 'brain storms' brought on by exam nerves; seduced by the glamour of London and fashion while making ends meet; wanting to be a buyer; then wanting to be the best buyer; winning over sceptical buyers when now a marketer; an immensely loyal and attractive first 'real' boyfriend yet an early divorce; the trauma and consequences of losing my next husband, Mike, at an early age; coping with the kids afterwards, while trying to cope myself with the devastating loss are all major life events that have moulded me into the hardworking woman I am today. I learned how to be there for my children as time gradually healed the wounds to find a 'new normal'.

No one is pretending that these events are easy to overcome. Neither the life-changing challenges nor the more normal ones that a lot of successful women find in business as they balance doing the best for their family with the needs and desires of wanting to succeed in work. But I have overcome them, largely with my femininity and good grace intact and without, most of the time, having to resort to putting the 'mask' on to succeed.

This sense of 'I am going to show them' is a regular theme and comes across many times during my story, but for me to really show them I need all the above key behaviours within the roots of my personal spirit to be both active and in balance.

Lose the context, and the security goes. Lose that and the intuitive radar, that is so often key when making 'big' decisions, loses direction. Then confidence in my own ability quickly drops.

Knowing when to move on has been characteristic in both my business and my personal life. When I felt the time was right to move away from my first real job as a Buyer for Harvey Nichols and the 'Knightsbridge Bubble', I went to the marked contrast of Tesco to broaden my buying skills. The opportunity to understand and engage with the McKinsey way in BHS enabled me to kick-start a move away from 'What' people buy in buying roles to 'Why' people buy and the world of the customer and brands. This led to a fantastic business turnaround in Early Learning Centre based on the principle of 'enriching the lives of children'. More recently I embraced the amazing experience of 'unleashing our customers' sexual confidence' at Ann Summers and of being part of a family affair in a role that was less a job and more about playing a part in the world of the family! My winning moments tend to take place when I see and wrap my head around the broader picture.

For me the parallel between personal and business relationships is obvious. In fact I don't see a distinction between the two and this has become even more so recently as I've stepped out of my corporate career to find my inner entrepreneur and to find more ways to give back. When it comes to looking at what makes a strong brand and successful company, I believe it is all about people; their values, beliefs and their relationships with the people who matter most to the business – their customers.

For me there is no difference between the brand and the company/business. They are mutually complimentary elements, parts of a whole. You cannot have a great company without a strong brand. If a company doesn't view its choices through the brand lens, contradictions and lack of clarity result. Increasingly in this world of rapid change and instantaneous communication through social media, a business that is unclear about its 'Why' is quickly uncovered. The days when a business could behave differently on the inside than the claims that it made to the outside world are long gone. If there is a difference in the way you treat your colleagues and the way you want your customers to be treated, this will translate with instant transparency through the experience your customers receive. Without a doubt, this approach has never been a recipe for creating the strongest connection with your customer, but the speed with which a business can unravel has never been more rapid than when trust is compromised.

So is that all there is to it? Not quite. Next we will explore your relationship with your customer. How do you create the connection? The answer is that the strongest brands create a compelling, emotional connection with their customers. While they may well be selling products or services that are justified by the customer on a rational basis of functionality, price, etc., the relationship with the brand is an emotional one. To put it another way, 'What' people buy is decided by 'Why' people buy. The first is rational, the second is emotional. It is a biological fact that the part of the brain controlling the emotions is where decisions are made (however much we might like to think otherwise)!

Brands that build an emotional bond play a significant role in the lives of their customers. This is about having a 'Why' that is important to your customers. It requires an understanding of their lives as well as their emotions. We need to know how their emotions translate into behaviour. We need to keep pace with, or preferably stay ahead of, our customers. I've been inspired by Simon Sinek, who describes this compellingly in his TED talks – as the business 'Why'. Many businesses overlook the importance of determining the 'Why' of their business. Most businesses understand the 'What' and the 'How', but without a clear 'Why' the potential for the business will be constrained and its long-term growth is likely to be in question. Without the context of the brand's 'Why' the business lacks the focus to deliver on its promise. Furthermore, it will find it very tricky to maintain the creativity necessary to evolve the business model to keep pace with the fast-changing needs of its customers. The business's 'Why' sets the standard by providing the context and tone for all decision-making. Additionally, the 'Why' guides the values, behaviours, communication, experience and even the measurement criteria for the business.

When a business has its 'Why' clearly defined, together with a determination to stay closely connected to its customers and understand what is going on in their lives, the possibilities are endless. The opportunity to continuously deliver on the brand promise while evolving the business model is there.

I love the story of The Discovery Channel. The leadership team understood their 'Why', to provide exciting, mind-expanding information about the world and nature in a relevant format. Originally the medium for such knowledge was encyclopaedias, but this forward-thinking team recognised that the business model needed to change. The brand 'Why' remained consistent, but the business model needed to evolve, and they did so with exciting results.

Contrast this exciting story with the less inspiring stories of Blockbuster and HMV. Both companies were in the media business with (potentially) strong brands. However, neither company could evolve their business models. Both were stuck doing the same things in the same ways while hoping for a different result. Their customers largely moved on and the only option they could see was to discount the product more and more heavily. They entered into a spiral of decline and the rest is history!

Another really important factor that I have not yet mentioned is leadership. Great brands tend to be led by great leaders. What makes a great leader? My personal experience is that great leaders, having ensured they have the right people around them, have trust in their team members. As a result of knowing they are trusted, people feel confident to step out of their comfort zones to make brave decisions where necessary. Energy levels remain high, even when the going gets tough, as they work together towards a shared vision and agenda.

An inspirational members' organisation for board and senior women working in retail is Women In Retail. My time spent working with Women In Retail has shown me just how crucial it is that women have leadership roles within customer-facing businesses in which women are the target customers. Did you assume this was already the case? Isn't it surprising that women fill only 15% of Board places in UK retail businesses? How can that make sense? Where women are in such a minority and yet the majority of purchase decisions are made by women, how can there be so few women in leadership roles, especially when retail also employs so many women?!

How can a board that is 85% male make purchase decisions for clients they may struggle to relate to? Pure logic suggests that it is nonsensical to have so few women in the boardroom for an industry that caters to women. If more women were in these boardrooms, things would be much better internally and commercially. It is crucial to place the right skills with the right approaches in leadership teams to achieve the best outcomes.

Simon Sinek, in another of his TED talks, tells us that great leaders make people feel safe. This feeling of safety is about trust acquired by demonstrating motivation, good judgment and competence. The leader must be trusted by those he is leading; he must also be able to trust those he is leading. Sinek refers to some amazing examples of tremendous selflessness of military leaders in the face of great danger, where they put the safety of the men under their command first. In one case, a military leader was described returning to the danger zone repeatedly to rescue as many of his men as possible with no concern for his own safety.

Another remarkable example demonstrates the importance of a leader's determination and resilience, but also their capacity to pace themselves and their teams while keeping the goal firmly in mind. The case study of Amundsen and Scott in 1911/12 in their quest to reach the South Pole has been widely researched and commented on over the years. Both led their teams to the South Pole while facing great odds, arriving within a month of each other. Amundsen led his team home successfully with no casualties. Sadly, Scott and all his team members perished on the return route. There were a number of differences in their approach, but the one that seems to have made the greatest difference is what has subsequently been described as the "Twenty Mile March Principle". For his team, Amundsen set a daily goal of covering twenty miles irrespective of conditions. They paced themselves accordingly and made consistent progress while managing to retain their energy levels and motivation. Scott, on the other hand, drove his team much harder when the conditions allowed it, but retreated to camp when the weather deteriorated. It seems that Scott's approach cost his team time, energy and motivation. The disparity between approaches appears to be a significant factor in the sharp contrast in the outcomes for the two teams.

Not all of us find ourselves in such extreme life or death leadership situations. However, many more of us will face choices as leaders, or work in situations where leaders have challenging choices to make. Frequently, it is when faced with a challenging market and disappointing business performance that a leader is most tested. When the obvious response may be to cut costs, it is the brave and visionary leader who faces the challenge with a more creative and inspiring set of solutions.

For example, there was a business owner who was advised to reduce headcount, but he refused to do so. Instead, he was open with his employees about the challenges facing the business and asked them all to consider taking unpaid leave to avoid the necessity of redundancies. Every employee agreed to the proposal, allowing the entire company to work together to share the spread of increased leave and reduced salary. In this way, people who could afford the most supported those who could afford the least. No one lost his or her job; the business turned around and, ultimately, thrived. Needless to say, this business owner was supported by a highly committed team of employees who worked together to grow the business following the turnaround.

In addition to trust, resilience and determination, a successful leader must have passion. During her early days at Burberry, Angela Ahrendts submitted her business plans to the Burberry advisors who suggested it would take up to three years to achieve her goals, if they could be achieved at all. "The goals I set were achieved in one year." She said afterwards that the factor the consultants hadn't considered was – Energy! The entrepreneurial leadership team at Innocent Drinks talks about being passionate from day one about working with people who share their values. Listening to their story was a stand-out moment for me. From the early days when they asked the public to vote as to whether they should continue their day jobs or take their brand forward, the original team of three knew what they were looking for in their working relationships. To this day, they invest significant time and resources in recruiting and retaining the right people. In their own words, they prefer to have 'a hole than an asshole'!

Much study and research has been done on the topic of successful leadership. A great leader is resilient, curious, and constantly striving to be better. At risk of oversimplifying this critical issue, I will put forward my perspective, which has been accumulated from my own experiences and listening to the views and experiences of others. I am writing this chapter from Cape Town, South Africa, where I spend a lot of time when I'm not in London. It strikes me that the much-loved and celebrated Nelson Mandela, who passed away in 2013, demonstrated all of the characteristics listed below. Do you agree?

- Confident, good self-esteem
- Sufficient humility to recognise he doesn't have all the answers
- Emotionally intelligent and a great listener (to colleagues and customers)
- Sets stretching but realistic goals
- Recognises and celebrates achievement
- Accepts responsibility, never completely satisfied
- Keeps asking questions
- Takes people with them

Last year I attended a two-day seminar on leadership through horse whispering. The principles of horse whispering came from some wonderful work by Monty Roberts. The Horse Whisperer, a movie starring Robert Redford based on the book of the same name by Nicholas Evans, utilises the principles of natural horsemanship (whispering) techniques. Steadily, much of the horse world has grown to embrace a kinder, more persuasive, more effective approach to training horses. Natural Horsemanship is now widely accepted and is endorsed by the Queen, a great lover of horses and an enthusiastic rider and owner herself. Monty clearly demonstrated that horses respond to the carrot rather than the stick. He showed that he could achieve in only 30 minutes an acceptance of the saddle, rather than the traditional style of training or 'breaking in' a horse. The metaphor is clear; horses and people respond to trust and rapport being developed rather than an approach of command and control. When I went horse whispering, I was in the process of setting up my new business and I realised that I needed to translate my leadership style into a new context. While the work that I would be doing would be influenced by my previous experience, I was hoping to learn how I might adapt my approach in different situations.

I quickly learned that I had to understand the horse's perspective along with the fact that I communicate quite a bit without words. We all do this whether we realise it or not. Horses respond to great leaders who they trust. A horse does not care about your job title or how much money you made last year; a horse cares about your confidence which is relayed through your body language. Caesar and Rolex were selected as partners for my learning experiences!

On the first day of the seminar I worked with Caesar; he was an older horse who thought he knew it all. I was told that he was a bit cynical and it might take time for him to trust me. I knew I would have to prove myself before he trusted or respected me. The course leaders were Hilary, an amazing horsewoman who understands people, along with Marie, an experienced and accredited business coach who understands horses, and Sammy, their colleague. They gave me my brief. Their advice was to first spend a little time getting to know Caesar, building trust and rapport. I had never been in a ring with a horse and this mature horse was going to need to take my lead! I needed to demonstrate a confidence that I may or may not have felt and I knew I also needed to be authentic or he would see me coming a mile off! This mature and experienced horse was used to doing things his way and I needed to convince him that he should follow me. In other words, I needed him to see that it might be worth thinking differently. Are you getting the metaphor for my work with people? I was about to receive the purest and most honest feedback possible.

Initially he wanted to take the lead and for me to follow him. However, I quickly, through gentle but firm persuasion, managed to get him to trot and canter around the ring in response to my signal. I even enticed him to come towards me on his own. This mature horse was prepared to change his behaviour in response to my convincing him there was another way and that I might be worth listening to! I was thrilled and couldn't wait for my next exercise. I'd also developed a real affection for Caesar. During this session, I learned much by watching other people's experiences, which were equally fantastic. One lady was truly terrified of horses, yet she managed to overcome this and learned loads about herself and others, too. Wonderful!

I met Rolex on the second day. He was much younger and extremely energetic, although he lacked confidence and had a lot to learn. At the same time, he was likely to be quite quick to trust, as he hadn't faced many challenges in his young life. He was a valuable horse and knew he was something special! Rolex was a truly beautiful horse. He was young and becoming a successful racehorse. It was evident to me that he was viewed as a bit of a star, but it hadn't gone to his head. I was told he was likely to be open to learning new things, but that he would need to feel very confident in me if he were to step out of his comfort zone! Are you getting the metaphor for people here?

After I introduced myself to Rolex and got to know him a little, I was told I was going to be given some challenges for us both, but it wasn't until after we had achieved everything that my guides told me that he had never done any of these things before! Initially, long pieces of wood were placed in the ring and I was tasked with building Rolex's confidence in me so that he would step over the pieces of wood. Much to my delight, and his too, I think, we were able to accomplish this! Then we were presented with a trickier task. A large, blue, plastic sheet was laid on the floor of the ring. The sheet represented water to Rolex and it was completely unfamiliar to him. A horse invariably prefers not to cross water. Rolex was further stymied because he had no idea how deep the 'water' was. We worked on getting familiar with the 'water' by getting closer to it and then I took the initial 'plunge' by stepping into the 'lake'. After a while Rolex followed me across! I was then asked to persuade Rolex to walk backwards, which is an unnatural movement for a horse. Not only did we manage this feat, but he even crossed our blue, plastic lake in reverse. Honestly, I felt close to tears; it was such a moving experience!

I will never forget my wonderful new friends, Caesar and Rolex, and the lessons they taught me about people, relationships, leadership and, of course, these beautiful creatures. I managed to build a wonderful rapport with both horses by the end of our sessions. I felt we'd become friends and I was very fond of each one. The exercises I was given to encourage the horses to take my lead were a wonderful metaphor for everyday life and leadership situations. The seminar made me realise just how influential non-verbal communication is! There were several examples of my horses accomplishing things with me for the first time; it was an amazing, inspiring, emotional, and confidence-building experience! As with horses, it is not your name or your title that people respond to; rather it is what you convey and the confidence you exude that inspires people to invest in you.

To summarise this part of my story, without the 'Why', the 'What', and the 'How' your business model will be unclear and you will not create a strong connection with your customers. Over time, your business model may need to evolve. If you are inattentive to changing trends, you may not notice that your customers have moved on and your business is standing still. Make a choice to be on a winning team to develop a clear and compelling 'Why'. Translate this into a 'WOW' customer experience by listening to your customers every day and being ready to innovate in order to evolve. You must be prepared to meet the changing needs of your customers, as well as continue to meet their current needs.

"They will forget what you said, they will forget what you did, but they will never forget how you made them feel." - Maya Angelou, poet.

Chapter 2
Some of the Great Love Affairs

Some of the brands we are in love with are long-standing and established; we have loved them for years. The love affair with these established brands is one of trust, confidence and aspiration; this affair has endured through the years. This love affair remains dependable. Dependable love does not mean a stagnant relationship! Rather, these brands have stood the test of time and continue to flourish because they are always in tune with the role they play in their customers' lives.

These brands are constant in our lives because they remain relevant. How do they remain relevant? They constantly assess and anticipate the changing needs of their customers. To do this, they must know their customer. Let's take a look at several long-standing brands that are excelling in their love affairs with their customers.

Nike is one brand that we have had a long-standing love affair with. This company was created by two men who knew running; one was a track coach and the other a middle-distance runner. They had the advantage of knowing their customers' needs from the inception of their brand because they were creating products for themselves!

The Nike 'swoosh' and 'Just Do It' motto are known worldwide. It is the go-to brand for stylish sportswear. Many pro athletes wear Nike gear; subsequently, it translates as the brand for achievers that offers a premium sportswear experience. A beginner dons Nike clothing, then looks and feels like a world class athlete before he ever hits the gym! Advanced athletes know they can depend on Nike attire, shoes and accessories because the Nike products have never let them down over the years. Additionally, Nike is aware of changing trends in exercising and is quick to offer products for those new trends. At first, Nike only offered running shoes, but now offers shoes for a variety of athletic endeavours.

BMW also offers variety to its customers. Established in 1916, BMW creates beautifully designed automobiles and motorcycles. The German engineering produces superb quality and stylishness. BMW is leading the pack when it comes to offering customisation for its customers. The leaders at BMW have created flexibility in the manufacturing of their cars so that as each car is being built, it is easy to customise. If a customer makes a change, it can be accommodated within several days rather than several months. BMW is tuned in to the changing needs of its customers and is rising to the challenge of offering customised luxury in a timely manner.

The extension of the BMW brand to underpin the quality and credentials of today's MINI is an exciting case study in its own right. I'll declare my bias here; I was the loving owner of two Minis until I embraced London life and realised that with such amazing public transport, I really didn't need a car! My first Mini was cream, my second was pale blue, both colours 'borrowed' from the Mini's original 1960s colour palette. Could Mini have added a welcome lightness of touch, a little femininity, playfulness as well as a touch of 'Britishness' to this iconic, confident, stylish yet rather masculine brand? I think so. BMW grants a luxurious, custom-built means of travel. Next we'll explore a brand that makes you look amazing while travelling.

Louis Vuitton is a brand with a long and authentic heritage in beautiful travel products that were originally more like travelling wardrobes. Louis Vuitton began making trunks in 1837 and opened his fashion house in 1854. At one time, Louis Vuitton was the largest travel goods store in the world. As travel needs changed, so did the offerings of the Louis Vuitton brand. This brand symbolises pure luxury.

While the brand's heritage is from a more leisurely and glamorous era, it is a brand that taps into its heritage to inform its position in the contemporary world, making it every bit as desirable as ever. Today, the company makes everything from trunks and leather goods to ready-to-wear attire, shoes, watches, jewellery, accessories, sunglasses, and books. The iconic Louis Vuitton logo is recognised worldwide. The brand extensions have been carefully managed to avoid stretching the brand too far beyond its original values, always reinforcing the aspirational cues of the brand.

Prada, like Louis Vuitton, began by selling luxury travel items. Both of these companies have remained current by changing their offerings while maintaining the luxurious quality of their brand. Prada launched in 1913 and initially sold Italian leather goods and imported trunks. As luxury travel became centred on air travel, heavy, bulky luggage lost its appeal, so Prada began making lightweight cases and handbags.

In 1919 Prada was appointed Official Supplier to the Italian Royal Household; as such, it was entitled to incorporate the House of Savoy's coat of arms and knotted rope design into its logo. Later, Prada became known for utilising innovative materials to create handbags that were unique and highly desirable.

Quality and innovation, as well as the respect for tradition, have always been the values Prada has subscribed to. While consistently adopting a cutting-edge approach in experimenting with new production techniques, new technologies and new fabrics, Prada has been able to harmonise this innovative approach while maintaining its very strong ties with tradition for craftsmanship and manual processes.

Prada was the first label, back in 1978, to use a particular type of nylon made of a fine, twisted weave, appearing as precious as silk, obtained through a special chassis. A new fabric trend was created in the world of fashion! (Source: Prada Group).

In 1977, Miuccia Prada, granddaughter of founder Mario Prada, along with Italian businessman Patrizio Bertelli, started their partnership and reinvigorated the brand. Just two years later Prada began its first line of women's shoes. Soon after, Prada launched stores around the world. The first women's clothing line ran in 1988, with a men's line following a few years later.

For those of us who love the Prada brand it needs no explanation. People adore shopping Prada for a fabulous and timeless handbag or purse, or perhaps a pair of sunglasses, a stunning pair of shoes, or, on a very rare occasion, a timeless piece of clothing that can be worn year after year.

There are now four brands under the Prada Group umbrella: Prada, Miu Miu, Church's, and Car Shoe. Miu Miu was founded in 1993 as a playful, sensuous and somewhat rebellious take on fashion. The brand name, Miu Miu, encompasses the playfulness of the brand – Miu Miu is Miuccia Prada's family nickname! This brand plays by mixing traditional with modern, masculine with feminine, elegance with experimentalism – you get the idea! It's founded on the principle of "playing around" with ideas. Miuccia Prada is synonymous with her brand, representing statement Italian styling with understated elegance.

The Prada brand embraces minimalism with an understated chic sophistication. The Prada duo explain how they have sustained and perfected their brand: "Careful observation of and curiosity about the world, society, and culture are at the core of Prada's creativity and modernity. This pursuit has pushed Prada beyond the physical limitations of boutiques and showrooms, provoked an interaction with different and seemingly distant worlds, and introduced a new way to create a natural, almost fashionless fashion." (Source: Prada Group). Well said!

Burberry is the final long-standing brand that I will mention. It is a stunning case study! Burberry was founded in 1856 by Thomas Burberry, a twenty-one year old dressmaker. Burberry supplied clothing and tents for arctic expeditions in the early 1900s. WWI officers, motorcyclists, aviators, skiers along with other adventurers wore Burberry outerwear. The Burberry trench became quintessential with English style.

Then, this heritage English brand became wildly over-exposed, resulting in a dramatic decline in credibility, aspiration and commercial results. Under Angela Ahrendts and Christopher Bailey the turnaround was spectacular and achieved in record time, returning the brand to its pinnacle status. It's clear that the two leaders were a fantastic yin and yang working together.

Angela, in one of her Ted Talks, spoke emotionally about the leadership style that enabled her and Christopher Bailey, in partnership, to achieve this. She related that the regrowth was all about people, belief, energy and a balance of right and left-brain thinking, as well as much more I'm sure!

We've explored premium brands that have stood the test of time. Now, let's consider a more accessible brand, Ikea. In the 1940's, Ingvar Kamprad used monies earned for good grades in school to begin his business. IKEA originally sold pens, wallets, picture frames, table runners, watches, jewellery and nylon stockings as Kamprad strove to meet needs with products offered at reduced prices. Over time, furniture, crafted by local artisans using wood from forests close to Kamprad's home, was added to the collection. A catalogue was later introduced and Ikea became a well-established brand. It is now the 'go to' brand for modern, stylish, well-designed, affordable furniture and furnishings.

I still remember one of their earlier ad campaigns: There was a large smile pictured and we were encouraged to 'chuck out our chintz'! I vividly remember anything flowery or ornate being thrown out of a house in favour of clean, simple lines. Just as importantly, they make furniture and a room makeover available when we want it at a price that we can afford. Previously, we needed a mortgage and a lot of patience to achieve the same thing! The Ikea proposition is as relevant today as in their earlier days.

The brands we've just studied are excellent examples of how important it is to know the needs and desires of customers. All of these brands demonstrate proactive planning and moving forward with their products and branding. Confidence and willingness to evolve the brand to fit the changing times is a hallmark of these brands.

Other brands we love have only emerged recently. This love affair is fresh and exciting, while also conveying long-term dependability and steadfastness. These brands moved in fast and shook up the marketplace. Let's take a look at how they managed to earn coveted spots at the top of people's minds.

We'll begin with Dyson. In 1978, James Dyson became frustrated with the poor performance of vacuum cleaners and realised that the vacuum cleaner bag was causing the vacuum to lose suction and perform poorly. He put his training as an industrial designer and inventor to work and soon created the first bagless vacuum cleaner. Dyson's highly innovative approach to product design and to the market is very much admired.

In a world where the vacuum cleaner had become synonymous with the brand Hoover, Dyson was unafraid to approach the product design and market from a new angle; as a result, he transformed the market. Dyson has become the brand of choice in most public loos, hotels, restaurants and offices.

Similarly, Nestlé Nespresso is another brand that capitalised by using technology. Nestlé Nespresso was founded in 1986 as a revolutionary system of perfectly portioned, encapsulated coffee. Nespresso offers coffees, coffee machines and chocolates. Nespresso has grown with the advent of new technology to now offer their product in a variety of formats. Their products may be purchased via telephone, their website and they even have a mobile app for ordering on the go.

Recently, Nespresso came under fire from an environmental perspective because of their single-use aluminium pods. Some feel that the pods create unnecessary waste. It is not known how many of Nespresso's pods end up in landfills versus the number that are recycled. Nespresso conducted its own research and found that instant coffee "uses less energy and has a lower environmental footprint than capsule espresso coffee or drip filter coffee, the latter having the highest environmental impacts on a per cup basis". (Source: The Guardian). Additionally, Nespresso claims a commitment to supporting the development of appropriate schemes to recover and recycle small aluminium packaging, such as the Nespresso pods. Nespresso is listening to their naysayers and responding by taking the concerns seriously. Bravo!

Nespresso has opened Boutiques that offer all of the services of the Nespresso Club in stylish surroundings. Opening the Boutiques has made coffee sexy in a new way. With George Clooney as their ambassador, their sexy 'edge' is clear from the start. People go into these stores to absorb the atmosphere and be seen. The brand, store and packaging design are synonymous with a highly premium brand experience; it is as far away from the volume experience of Starbucks or Costa as it is possible to be. Nespresso is the Prada of coffee!!!

Not every company relies on sex or luxury to market their brand. Innocent, founded in 1999, has rewritten the rules. Three young Cambridge graduates who were just beginning in their respective careers decided to create a new product range of healthy, natural, 'innocent' juices, which they initially sold at concerts and weekend festivals. They asked the public to vote as to whether they should keep their day jobs or take Innocent forward. Only three people voted for them to keep their day jobs – and it turns out they were their parents! (Source: Innocent Drinks).

While it was far from plain sailing for these guys, they kept going and the brand went from strength to strength. Innocent now produces veg and noodle pots, smoothies, juices, including a juice line for children. The Innocent brand is stocked in major supermarkets including Waitrose and is sold in fifteen European countries.

In 2013, Coca Cola gained 90% of the company and will take the brand worldwide while still maintaining the ethical vision of the three original founders. The founders of Innocent took a risk when they began their brand.

We mentioned Ikea as a long-standing furniture brand that has stood the test of time. I'd also like to mention another furniture company that is newer to the market that I believe will also stand the test of time. Warren Evans is a craftsman furniture brand. Their products are built to order and delivered within about a week, which is quite incredible. The wood is FSC (Forest Stewardship Council). The people who deliver are kind and courteous and build the furniture in the location of your choice; after which they take away all the packaging and you are left admiring your great choice. The furniture is stylish, affordable, great quality, space saving, personal and personable. What more could we want? I now have a Warren Evans bed in three out of four bedrooms as well as two wardrobes and a chest of drawers. I wouldn't go anywhere else now!

I'd also like to mention another brand I admire. This happens to be a brand I've personally worked with. The Christopher Ward luxury watch company was founded in 2004 by Mike France, Chris Ward and Peter Ellis. Right from the start the business purpose has always been about finding a way for everyone to enjoy the truly visceral pleasure derived from owning and wearing a premium quality Swiss-made watch, especially one where the value for money is without question. (Source: christopherward.com). Christopher Ward has been putting premium, Swiss-made watches within the reach of everyone for over 10 years now.

Christopher Ward has a unique business model, putting the customer in direct contact with the watchmaker. They handle the direct selling of their watches, rather than relying on third party retailers. You can buy online or visit their showroom by appointment for a truly personalised experience. Additionally, they operate on fair margins resulting in honest pricing. They choose not to endorse their brand or product with celebrities or sponsorships. Isn't this interesting? Celebrity endorsements almost guarantee sales, but Christopher Ward knows just how costly it is to hire celebrities. And they know who ultimately pays that cost. The enormous cost to hire a celebrity to endorse the product would ultimately be passed on to the customer in the form of higher-priced merchandise. They believe their customers are wise enough to recognise quality without the aid of a celebrity. Finally, their customer care is unrivalled and their guarantee is unmatched. Their customer service method relies on respect, courtesy and common sense. It is borne of an acknowledgement that their success is entirely dependent on the satisfaction and delight of their customers. (Source: christopherward.com).

Next, we'll take a look at a company that took a risk, as well, by moving into a possibly over-saturated market. Would it succeed? Superdry was conceived in 2003 by Julian Dunkerton and James Holder. The urban street-wear, which was sold in Cult Clothing stores, was moving into the over-supplied casual clothing market where it might have been difficult to imagine another successful player. This was not the case with Superdry! By 2012, the success of Superdry led management to rebrand its Cult stores into Superdry stores. Superdry is now sold in over 100 countries worldwide.

The founders remain active members of the business; additionally, the business is led by a capable, experienced leadership team. It seems the vision and values of the creators of Superdry remain focused while embracing new thinking, too.

Another brand that embraces new thinking is Seraphine. This is a wonderful maternity brand set up by Cecile Renaud, a charming and stylish French lady. She has created a brand where the collection is so stunning that women who are not pregnant find the clothes just as appealing as those who are! Seraphine describes themselves as the International Brand of Choice for pregnancy fashion. They certainly do seem to be just that if their growth is anything to go by. Additionally, they have an impressive celebrity following, including the Duchess of Cambridge!

Cecile had the vision to enter this market when the established brands were looking tired. She approached her plans with fresh eyes and the result has been amazing. She is now introducing a children's range of clothing. She is a challenger and an entrepreneur to be admired, having won the Queen's Award for Enterprise in 2015!

While not so much a challenger brand, Ted Baker is a wonderful case study of a confident fashion brand for men and women. This brand is clearly and firmly led by its founder, the famously camera shy Ray Kelvin, who conceived the idea while fishing in 1987. In 2011, Ray Kelvin was awarded a CBE by Her Majesty Queen Elizabeth for services to the fashion industry, and, subsequently, in 2014 Ray Kelvin received the accolade from Retail Week for his outstanding contribution to retail. This is the retail equivalent of the Oscars in the UK and reflects the industry admiration for the way that the Ted brand has evolved and developed its unique and quirky handwriting, while successfully stretching the brand into associated brand extensions and spreading the brand internationally. Kelvin is surrounded by a loyal team that is balanced with fresh, contemporary thinking. He clearly listens to his team and then the business moves forward with a clear vision for the future.

We have discussed many successful premium brands. But there are many brands that are more accessible to all that are enjoying great success as well. Primark opened its first store in Dublin in 1969. They now have stores located throughout Europe and are beginning to launch in the United States. The Primark brand aims to 'offer the lowest prices on the high street.' They accomplish this by shying away from high-priced ad campaigns, preferring to allow their customers to do the selling for them. They encourage customers to post pictures on the store website showing how they've styled their Primark purchases. This brand is wildly popular. Everyone can shop Primark and look fashionable!

Many people are shopping differently today. The growth of brands at the lower priced end of the mark is demonstrative of this difference in shopping. Once upon a time a Waitrose customer only shopped at Waitrose. Now Waitrose customers are also shopping at Aldi and Lidl for their groceries. Both Aldi and Lidl offer a different way of shopping to keep costs down and customers are embracing it!

Conversely, let's explore a brand that did have huge success, but did not have the benefit of a team or a vision for the future. Flappy Birds was an overnight success. In just a few weeks the mobile app became a worldwide phenomenon. The success of this brand crept up on everyone, including the creator! This game is a great example of how a product can have immediate success due to word-of-mouth, accessibility and desire. The sudden success followed by its equally sudden removal from the marketplace makes this a bittersweet story.

At the end of January 2014, it was the most downloaded free game in the iOS App Store. During this period, its developer claimed that Flappy Bird was earning $50,000 a day from in-app advertisements as well as sales. It was pulled from the marketplace in February 2014, because the creator felt it was too addictive. It remains unclear whether this was the true cause or whether there were looming legal issues.

Flappy Birds was eventually re-released to the delight of its fans. This extraordinarily controversial brand is a prime example of a desirable product making the big time. It is also an example of how important good leadership and vision are to the sustainability of a brand.

An exploration of brands that have entered into the social media market would not be complete without considering two of the biggest players. Google and Facebook are both clearly in the category of challenger brands that have now become so much a part of all of our lives that we can barely remember life without them. The terms 'Google it' and 'Facebook generation' have been grafted into our vocabulary; these brands allow us to share information and interact with others in a way that was never before possible. These brands have defined our approach and access to communication and information.

Then, there are brands that we love from afar because we are not sure of them. We want to love them, but will they stand the test of time?

Mojo Motion: To develop a great love affair with your customers that will stand the test of time, remain one step ahead. Remain relevant, yet dependable, by always knowing the changing needs of your customers. If you do this, they cannot help but fall in love with you!

Chapter 3
How Fast Can You Fall (Out of Love)?

Imagine a love affair that ended badly. At the beginning of this love affair you admired your love interest. There were all sorts of lovely feelings for this person. Then, your love did something wrong; they behaved badly, made a poor choice, hurt your feelings or damaged your perception of them in some way. Suddenly, this person no longer garnered those lovely feelings from you. Your memories are now tarnished and your perception of your lover is no longer one of admiration, but one of disappointment and, possibly, harsh judgment.

Now let's apply these feelings to a brand and take a look at how quickly people's perception of a brand can change for the worse. There are many people who are their own brand; this is the personality, or celebrity, brand concept. We will examine some individuals who have damaged their personal brands significantly. The fascinating aspect of this exploration is that some have recovered their reputations (brands) while others have not. We will explore the reasons for the different outcomes.

We start with a notorious individual, OJ Simpson. Once known as "The Juice", OJ Simpson is a retired American football player, broadcaster, actor and convicted felon who is currently in prison. During his football career he was highly regarded; after all, he was the first football player to rush for more than 2,000 yards in a season! He holds the record for the single season yards-per-game average and was elected into the Pro Football Hall of Fame in 1985. After his football career, he became a sports broadcaster and an actor, appearing in TV and films such as the miniseries Roots and the Naked Gun trilogy.

OJ Simpson was admired for his athletic ability, handsome looks, and his acting abilities. All of that changed abruptly in 1994 when he was arrested for double murder. Many people stood by "The Juice" and could not believe he would commit such an atrocious act. Others cut their ties of loyalty immediately.

The Trial of the Century, as it is known, ended with acquittal; but he was later found liable in a civil trial. In 2007, Simpson was arrested and charged with armed robbery and kidnapping; he was found guilty and is currently serving a prison sentence. However, people's loyalties are still divided over OJ Simpson. Some still defend him while others condemn him. Why? Issues of race and money were certainly underlying factors that contributed to a division of public opinion at the time of his conviction. These factors are still relevant to those who defend him.

Lance Armstrong is another notorious athlete who was once admired for his incredible athletic feats by winning the Tour de France a record seven times. Armstrong was considered to be especially accomplished athletically because he was also a cancer survivor. People admired him not only for his competitive cycling talents, but also for his dedication to helping others through his charity foundation, the Livestrong Foundation, which provides support for cancer patients.

In 2011, Armstrong retired from competitive cycling amidst a US federal investigation into allegations that he was using illicit performance-enhancing drugs. The court of public opinion quickly turned against Armstrong. Why?

Lance Armstrong's brand was all about clean living and sportsmanship as well as doing the right thing. He built his brand on trust. When this trust was broken, the public felt their sympathy and admiration for his achievement in recovering from cancer to become such a great sportsman had been badly misplaced. His response to this broken trust and his misdeeds seemed petulant, reinforcing the less positive aspects of his character. And we understand he has said "I would do it again."

Additionally, he allowed his girlfriend to say she was driving the car when he hit another car late at night, initially leaving the scene without reporting the accident. His attitude along with his actions cause him to come across as reluctant to learn from his mistakes and take responsibility for his actions. Because of this perception, public opinion has turned against him.

Oscar Pistorius is yet another athlete whose reputation became tarnished. At the 2011 World Championship in Athletics, Pistorius became the first amputee to win an able-bodied, world track medal. Pistorius became the first double leg amputee to participate in the Olympics in 2012. At the 2012 Summer Paralympics, Pistorius won gold medals, setting world records in both events. He also set a world record in the semi-final. Due to his unique talent, he had many sponsorship deals with Nike, Oakley and Thierry Mugler, to name a few.

In 2013, Pistorius shot and killed his girlfriend in his home; he was a hero turned villain overnight. He was convicted of the culpable homicide and is currently incarcerated. How has his brand been affected?

Pistorius went from hero to zero. One day he was the Olympic hero (Blade Runner), then on Valentine's Day 2013, he killed his beautiful, intelligent girlfriend of three months, Reeva Steenkamp. Of course his brand has been hugely affected by his actions. Nike suspended its contract with Pistorius shortly after the incident took place. It is unlikely his reputation is recoverable.

It is reported that he is advising fellow prisoners on diet and exercise and aiming to set up a sports club, so could it be that he will be given some credit if he handles his period in prison with dignity and a generosity of spirit towards others? Time will tell.

Arnold Schwarzenegger and Tiger Woods are two men who have many commonalities. They were both considered clean cut, family men who were married to beautiful women. Both committed adultery and were found guilty in the court of public opinion. One has been able to recover his brand while the other has not.

Let's explore the key differences between these two men. Arnold Schwarzenegger has more than one brand. In a sense, his movie characters are additional personas that the public see as being a part of Schwarzenegger himself. People think of Schwarzenegger as The Terminator and admire the character he played. He has been able to redeem himself, publicly, by relying on some of these movie characters.

Tiger Woods has one brand — himself. The brand Woods created for himself was one of a squeaky-clean, family man and excellent golfer. Tiger Woods was also the pinnacle of his profession; he was in a league with very few other athletes. When he became a professional golfer in 1996, he signed deals with Nike and Titleist, which were the most lucrative contracts in golf at that time. That same year he was named Sports Illustrated's Sportsman of the Year and the PGA Tour Rookie of the Year. Since that time he has been awarded PGA's Player of the Year a record eleven times. He was elevated on such a high pedestal that when he fell, he had a long way to fall. Why are people's expectations for these two men so different?

Arnold has been seen as a bit of a rough diamond, an alpha male. There is an element of macho maleness that makes his actions not so much okay, but somewhat more expected. It is not shocking to hear of someone with his personality and background behaving the way he did. Throughout his career he has encountered allegations of sexual misconduct; interestingly, these allegations did not hold The Terminator back. People have been accepting him as a "bad boy" for most of his career.

In contrast to Arnold, Tiger Woods was squeaky clean. He lost the clean-cut image when it became public knowledge that he was unfaithful to his beautiful wife. His profile was defined by the perspective of him being a loving husband and caring father to his lovely children, whom he was so often pictured with. The story of his adultery made him look less like a golf superstar and more a ridiculous married man caught with his pants down! Since this time his golf game has declined, which has not won him any new supporters.

Kate Moss is a world famous model who is still in high demand in her forties, an age when most models cannot find work. Not only is she tremendously desired as a representative for numerous premium brands, but she has managed to recover her position after a fall from grace.

In 2005, Moss lost prestigious sponsorships with H&M, Chanel and Burberry due to drug allegations. Even though she was caught on camera supposedly snorting cocaine, the allegations were dropped and Moss regained her career. In 2007, with estimated earnings of $9 million, she was the second highest paid model in the world, behind Gisele Bündchen.

Martha Stewart's brand is one of domestic perfection. She exemplifies hearth and home by selling the brand of hospitality, good food and comfortable, stylish surroundings. Stewart was convicted and jailed for insider trading, yet she emerged from prison a sympathetic figure. She, too, recovered and regained her career. Stewart has rebuilt herself many times before. She explained that her 2004 criminal trial "could've taken down the brand; it did not. But I must tell you that rebuilding is a lot harder than building." (New York Times).

According to The New York Times, her website continued to make huge gains in visitors in the coveted 18-to-34 demographic. Despite the fact that she had to eliminate two magazines from her publishing empire and the Hallmark Channel cancelled her show, major retailers battled over her in court because her name has never been worth more. The New York Times characterised it as "a schoolyard fight between two boys — the chief executives of Macy's and JC Penney— over the most popular girl on the playground."

Kate Moss and Martha Stewart are both examples of successful women with powerful brands who made grave mistakes that damaged their brands significantly. Both women have been able to recover their brands. How?

Kate Moss is unique. There is no other model who possesses the unique Kate style. As a result, she continues to be the muse, ambassador and representative of numerous high profile and aspirational brands. Ultimately it is as her own woman with her own unique approach to fashion and life that she is most admired. She comes across as a natural at what she does. She is photographed and followed for her own private 'take' on fashion and style, as well as in the role of 'the face of" famous brands. Her brand is as much about non-conformity as conformity to the fashion bible. Somehow she manages to combine looking classically beautiful with a naughty girl, rocker chic lifestyle. And we love her as much for this as her fashion 'icon' status. She's not perfect, but we love her for it!

Martha Stewart is a sympathetic figure. Many people felt she was being made a scapegoat; public opinion, therefore, was more sympathetic towards her position rather than towards the 'system'. It seems she was forgiven because her actions, although a significant mistake, did not inherently damage what she and her business stood for.

I think it would be interesting to reflect on Victoria and David Beckham as a positive example of celebrity branding. Their brand is strong and continues to evolve. David has gone from a world-class footballer to charity icon and force for good on a world stage. Victoria has gone from pop icon to celebrated fashion designer, recognised by the notoriously selective fashion world from Vogue and Anna Wintour along with many others. In addition, Victoria is beginning to adopt an increasingly philanthropic role in her own right. This couple is a great example of brands and individuals reflecting their purpose as the picture evolves while remaining highly topical, admired and newsworthy.

We have just explored how quickly people's perception of a brand, in this case the celebrity brand, can change for the worse. This can certainly happen with a business brand, as well. When establishing a business brand, you do not want to lose relevance or connection with your customers. You and your team will pursue relevance and connection by staying in touch with your customers' wants and needs. Of course, you will maintain the integrity of your business and your brand so that you never violate your customers' trust in you, your business or your brand.

Consider the pitfalls made by such companies as HMV and Blockbuster, who we've already discussed. A few other businesses who to varying degrees have lost their connection with their customer – Tesco, with significant questions related to their financial integrity; Gerald Ratner who showed a spectacular lack of respect for his customers and paid a high price and M&S, once the darling of the UK high street who despite us all willing them to succeed, seems to struggle to regain their touch. To avoid similar pitfalls, listen to your customers and respond to their needs. Always keep the future in mind. Stay relevant by knowing the brand today and how it engages with customers. Keep sight of how the business will need to evolve to remain topical and engage with tomorrow's customers.

Times have changed. You can no longer broadcast your brand as it is; rather, you need to engage with your customers. You have to converse with them, listening and responding. Always remember that the customer is in charge. When they talk, you listen. Also consider this: Who is your customer listening to?

Mojo Motion: Protect the integrity of your business and your brand. Never give your customers a reason to lose their trust in you, your business or your brand.

Chapter 4
The Heart of the Matter: Product to Desire

Which comes first, the product or the brand? People hold passionate views on this debate; however, the reality is that the product is what people take home with them, while the brand is the 'aura' that surrounds the product. If the two are not complimenting each other beautifully, the dissonance is obvious and both product and brand are compromised. If the product does not reflect and live up to the expectations set by the brand then both are undermined.

In our society, where brands prevail, very few people 'need' much at all. Yet, we can be influenced and persuaded to buy. More importantly, we can rationalise what we should buy, or post-rationalise to ourselves about what we have bought. Even where there is a need, such as when a car needs to be replaced or a washing machine has broken and the laundry is piling up, there are invariably, if not always, brand influences involved.

The brand halo, or aura, is key to our desire to purchase. Whether it is subtly or more overtly, subconsciously or consciously, there will be an element of the purchase being reinforced with the endorsement that the brand brings. What are customers looking for, what triggers them to buy, and what causes them to choose one brand over another? Price is, of course, a factor, but very few decisions are made purely on price. So what other factors come into play?

The price is justified in the context of the 'value ad' brought by the product attributes and the brand credentials. Ultimately, whether it is something we truly need or feel we just have to have, our hearts will beat faster and we will enjoy using that item on an on-going basis after purchase — as long as the product lives up to the promise of the brand. Ideally, we will wish to buy more products from this brand, whether new innovations of the same item or new products from the same brand. So how is this achieved?

In the fashion business, we talk a lot about 'product handwriting'. What do I mean by that? In simple terms, it is the style, the look, and the 'feel' of one brand over another. The range handwriting will tell a story and evoke a set of emotions through the shapes, fabrics used, and styling details. Through the combination of all these elements, the product will take on a recognisable look that reflects the brand and resonates with customers who are attracted to the brand.

Another way to look at this is if I removed all the distinguishing labels and explicit branding from a piece of clothing, could it be identified with its brand? What if you saw two identical dresses, one had the label of a designer you admire and the other did not? What would drive you to pay more for the dress with the label?

Product handwriting does not just apply to fashion. Think of the distinctive look and feel of an Apple device. Contrast this image with Samsung, for example. I'm sure for Samsung fans, the brand conjures up some strong values, but as I sit here writing I struggle to picture the product. Also, consider car brands; picture the curvy lines of an Audi TT versus a BMW Z4. Both cars are fast, sexy, beautifully designed and aesthetically pleasing. But their styles, or handwriting, are very different.

If the handwriting isn't reflective of the brand or distinctively recognisable, then your heart will not beat faster, you will question the price commanded and you will consider an alternative. This distinct product handwriting means that an item is recognisable at a distance and is distinguished as being superior to other similar products.

As customers, we prefer to believe that our choices are based on rational criteria, but are they? Product handwriting shapes how we feel about the product. What is it that we are taking home with us when we make such a purchase decision? It is more than just a pair of shoes, a blouse or a car. As well as having fallen in love with the product itself, we are taking the brand home with us; we've bought an item that we love and feel good about owning, which reflects the values of the brand. We feel we've made a good decision. If it is a fashion item, we will have felt amazing when we tried it on and we can't wait to wear it!

If it is a car, we are no longer simply driving from point A to point B. Our drive becomes an experience, an adventure! We look forward to driving it for the first time and notice other cars of the same brand and model on the road, which is likely to reinforce our decision. The relationship we have with the brand makes us feel we've made a good decision. Notably, wearing or using the item says something about ourselves, our personal style and our choices; we are making a statement of some kind, either to ourselves, others, or both, whether consciously or otherwise.

Brand relationship is key. Consider a phone. In the past, a phone was a tool used to make a call. We relied on it, but did not have much of a relationship with our telephone. Now, smartphones are intertwined in practically every aspect of our lives! Samsung sells more phones worldwide than Apple due to the popularity of its flagship smartphone, the Galaxy S series, as well as increased sales of lower-end models. However, Apple is the clear leader in the market for premium devices.

The first Apple computer was created in 1976 by Steven Wozniak and Steven Jobs, who were high school friends. By 1980, Apple had several thousand employees, mid-level managers, investors and was selling computers abroad. Twenty-five years later, in 2001, Apple spent a year penetrating the market with one million iPods. In 2014, it took six hours to sell one million iPhones in China alone! Forty percent of the world is now online and Apple has catered to that brilliantly. Apple understands that people are willing to pay for quality, premium phones. As a result, they do not discount their phones, which increases their standing as the go-to brand for a premium device. Our smart phones have more power than the original Apollo missions to the moon! The capability is overwhelming, yet potential for growth continues. Apple is a brand that knows how to think ahead and move one step ahead of their customers' needs.

Potentially controversial, Uber is an interesting case study that piggybacks on smartphones. This brand has captured the imagination of commuters around the world because it harnesses the use of smartphone technology to provide a service. Uber has created an app that makes it possible to quickly obtain a taxi service and pay for it so that you can quickly catch a ride without having to have cash on hand. Uber tracks the entire transaction, including tracking you while you travel with their driver so that your safety fears are mollified. What will the impact of Uber on the traditional taxicab business be? Uber's emergence and success has certainly disrupted the current market. Customers are now getting used to a higher level of service. It will be interesting to see how traditional taxicab brands adjust their model to capture lost customers.

In just five years, Uber has gone from zero to £27 billion valuation. It has even become a verb! We now Uber a ride, so they must be doing something right! Can you think of other brands that have become common nouns or verbs? If you are curious, why don't you google it? Google has dominated the Internet world and has been the search engine of choice so much so that it has become a verb, as well. Other common terms that are actually brands include these: Kleenex, Onesies, PowerPoint, Windbreaker, Hula Hoop, Frisbee, Styrofoam, Band-Aids, Velcro, Tupperware, Q-Tips, and Chapstick. This is only a sampling of the stellar brands that have remained at the apex of their market for many years.

From fashion to food we have become 'blended' shoppers, combining our priorities for style, quality, choice, price and convenience as we see fit. In other words, whether it is food or fashion we are considering, we are tending to shop in our own equivalent of Prada to Primark depending on our preferences and motivation.

We have explored the product and brand relationship as well as the concept of 'product handwriting', but what about choice and range? Brand owners do not want us to buy one item; they'd like us to buy several items from the range and/or come back again and again to buy more. To do this, the brand owners must offer 'real choice' within the range. They must make us feel that our needs and wants are being fulfilled. The range needs to speak to us in a way that is compelling; it needs to communicate that the range is what we need.

The range of products and choice needs to be coherent; we need to understand the 'look' and the 'story'. If an item stands out as not belonging, it can undermine the whole range and compromise the brand, leaving us feeling uncertain and, therefore, unlikely to buy. One item may not be a problem, but if the product handwriting becomes confused, then it certainly will be a problem, as customers we will begin to lose confidence and potentially go elsewhere. To some extent, this is what happened with Burberry when the brand values were undermined by incoherent and careless product development as well as an over-exposed brand. This was a trend that was spectacularly turned around by Angela Ahrendts and Christopher Bailey.

What are the factors that impact customers' choice and purchase decisions? Three factors we have explored are service, personalisation and trustworthiness. Let's start with service. We want our problems solved, immediately, cost effectively, and, most importantly, as promised. "Do not let me down!"

We want products and services that are designed to respond to our needs, so personalisation is an important trend. The product must convey that it is for me and about me. When I feel personally engaged with a brand, I will return to that brand's products and services over and over again.

Finally, we want our brand choices to represent good quality that we can trust. We expect our brand choices to be innovative, to be relevant and even a little ahead. Most importantly, the brands we purchase must keep their promises. The quality of the brand is paramount to its success. Brands have promises to keep to customers, colleagues, and to stakeholders. Failure to do this is spotted very quickly these days!

Mojo Motion: Authentic product handwriting will make your customers forget all other brands as they fall head-over-heels for your unique story. Your product handwriting will show a product with style, look and a feel that your customers desire.

Chapter 5
Customers Who Love You

What do your customers say when you are not in the room? Their relationship with your brand is not just about the product, but the experience they have in the store, restaurant, online, etc. The love your customers have for your product encompasses the connection and the experience they have over the transaction. In the past, the brand owner was able to control the image of the brand through advertising and other forms of public relations. Today, customers shape their view of a brand through social media. The world of advertising has changed significantly and the most successful brands embrace this style of advertising and public relations rather than try to staunch it.

Have you ever thought about how much information you are bombarded with each day? In 2013, a study showed that a typical user of social media consumes 285 pieces of content per day. This is equivalent to reading a novel a day or watching four Star Wars movies a day! To take in all of that information would take us twelve hours, or one-and-a-half workdays. Our brains are on constant overload from information bombardment. How customers make sense of this information is critical for you, the brand owner, to understand.

Take off your business owner hat for a few minutes and think like your customer. Your customer has to make sense of all the information they are receiving about your brand. It is their choice as to what information they decide to pull from what is being pushed at them. There is a new retail paradigm: The customers are in control, not the retailer.

Trip Advisor is an excellent example of this shift. In the past, we would use the Michelin Guide to determine which restaurants were worth visiting. In doing so, we were relying on "experts" to inform us. Today, we seek out this information from our peers via Trip Advisor. The customers are in control. They are empowered with knowledge gained from other customers. The customers are further in control because retailers know the customer's experience will likely end up on Trip Advisor, so customer service is at an all-time high. Customer reviews are powerful and can positively or negatively affect your brand.

Typically, two-thirds of the information a customer uses to evaluate a brand involves customer-driven marketing activities, such as customer reviews, word-of-mouth recommendations, or past experiences with the brand. Customers will pull positive information from retailers if they feel that the brand has a connection with them.

So, how can your brand rise above the information "noise" to be recognised? It is all about The Three E's: Engage, Equip and Empower. Engaging with your customer is very similar to engaging with people in your life on a personal level. How do you engage with friends? You reach out to them by being present in their lives. You talk to them and listen to them; you have a dialogue. Most interactions with close friends pick up right where they left off because you are tuned in to each other. This is the relationship you should have with your customers. The means of engagement are different, but the goals are the same. Whether you are listening to your customers on Trip Advisor, Twitter, Facebook or some other medium, you need to be a good listener.

In the digital age, this requires a new set of skills. It means listening to customers who are already having conversations about brands, yours and others, via online channels. Join these conversations and take part in a genuine and human way. Foster trust and form relationships through open, honest interactions. These relationships will develop over time, so be patient as you work to develop trust with your customers.

Engaging in interactions that create positive experiences and outcomes for your customers equips them. Positive outcomes include you being present to answer questions, solve problems, listen to ideas and support your customer. When a customer has been met with a proactive and positive response in this way, they are encouraged to feel increasingly warm about the relationship with the brand.

Recently, a friend of mine told me about her friend's yogurt experience. She found a slug in her yogurt. Ugh! Can you imagine her reaction? She instantly tweeted about her experience. Take off your customer hat for a moment and replace it with your retailer hat as you consider the nightmare this tweet could have been for the yogurt company. Within five minutes – five minutes! – the yogurt company contacted my friend and offered her a full refund and a gift certificate towards her next purchase, along with reassurance of the procedures in place to prevent this from happening again. The company listened, harnessed technology and retained a customer. In doing so, they equipped this customer. What I mean by 'equipped' is that they gave my friend a reason to speak positively about the good experience she had.

Other examples of equipping your customers involve giving them conversation starters through news stories, amazing facts, and state-of-the-art technologies. Apple carries this off in stellar fashion. Apple is constantly communicating and creating buzz about their new gadgets. Their customers carry on the buzz through all manner of communication by talking, tweeting or texting about Apple's newest designs or technologies. Apple seems to know what we want before we know that we want it. Would you have had the desire to adjust your home thermostat remotely with your iPhone if Apple had not brought the capability to you? We are growing in expectation that brands will anticipate our needs. Accordingly, you empower your customers by letting them have their say about your brand, whether it is recommendations, competitions or involvement in your brand.

If you make a customer happy, he will tell someone; if you make him unhappy he will tell ten people. This is word-of-mouth at its most basic. The theory behind the 1:10 ratio is that all businesses, regardless of size, are motivated to perform lest they risk a marketplace indictment by the judge and jury known as word-of-mouth. In this new age, online platforms have caused word-of-mouth to transform into a powerful dynamic called "user generated content" (UGC). This occurs when a customer posts online about her experiences, questions, praise or condemnation about a seller's products, services or general behaviour in the marketplace. To be colloquial, it is word-of-mouth on steroids. It is imperative that businesses focus on gathering loyal fans. If you don't yet believe me, consider the following:

- Fifty or more reviews per product can mean a 4.5% increase in conversion rates.
- 63% of customers are more likely to make a purchase from a site that has user reviews. (iPerceptions, 2011).
- Site visitors who interact with both reviews and customer questions/answers are 105% more likely to purchase while visiting, and spend 11% more than visitors who do not interact. (Bazaarvoice, Conversation Index, Q2, 2011).
- Consumer reviews are significantly more trusted, nearly twelve times more, than manufacturer descriptions. (eMarketer, February 2010).

- Customer reviews produce an average 18% increase in sales. (Reevoo).

Those are impressive statistics, aren't they? Consider Ben & Jerry's #CaptureEuphoria Instagram campaign which asked followers to submit an image that best depicted the joy of enjoying Ben & Jerry's. The prize? The winning images were used for custom-made ads with the original Instagram poster getting a nod. The company enjoyed a 22% increase in sales during this campaign! Another successful example is a campaign enacted by the Four Seasons Hotel. They ran several contests in cities such as Hong Kong and Toronto where customers were encouraged to take inspiring pictures that included specific landmarks of the city. The lucky winner of this contest received a weekend stay at the hotel. Think of your own experiences – what examples do you have where you feel brands have engaged, equipped and empowered you? Now, what can you do to take this concept forward in your own business?

Because the customer is subjected to so much information, the retailer must stand out from the rest. To do this, the message must be relevant and authentic. To be relevant, the brand must meet the customers where their needs are right now and look ahead to what their needs will be in the future. To be authentic, the brand must connect with their customers on an emotional level, engaging customers in the brand's story and ideals. This is a universal truth regardless of how you segment your customers. The way you speak to them and attempt to understand them must always be authentic, whether the customers are young, old, loyal, occasional or lapsed. Authenticity cannot be faked. It is a wholeness of purpose and action, which requires taking a stand for something beyond selling, then taking actions to prove it.

No one wants to be friends on social media with someone who constantly posts about their job. This holds true for brands, as well. A company who posts promotion after promotion will find their fan base dwindling. There is no authenticity in this. The key is to find something universal and true beneath the brand's product base or tagline and then create content that inspires those ideals. This type of content successfully connects with and engages your audience and will, ultimately, sell products.

For example, Red Bull sells consumers a belief in the extreme. Red Bull focuses on inspiring its audience with the essence of the brand, rather than pushing the product. In doing this, Red Bull creates authentic connections with its customers, who connect with the brand's image and share the brand's passion. Red Bull has created loyal fans while incorporating their energy drink into a symbol of their fans' energetic lifestyles. The Red Bull Stratos stunt is the most iconic example of this philosophy. A professional daredevil attempted a 128,000-foot free-fall to Earth from space. More than eight million people tuned in live, and more than thirty million people have viewed the stunt on YouTube.

Another great example I received recently was from Boden. They messed up by using a print advertisement that included a nude lady on the beach. As soon as this mistake was brought to their attention they apologised and used this as a motive to email their base with a quirky and fun message that was completely in keeping with their brand image and values. Authenticity in action!

Customers are adapting faster than some retailers because other retailers are anticipating our needs. As customers we are savvier and much better informed than in years past. Consider these three W's regarding your customers: When, What, and Where.

When: We expect the brands we love to always know what we need and supply it the moment we desire it. Amazon Prime guarantees delivery within 48 hours. Those who live in larger cities can order a product from various brands in the morning and have it delivered that afternoon. If you hear of a new book you would like to read, you can download it on an e-reader and begin reading immediately. The 'When' is now!

What: Customers want products and services to be meaningful on a personal level. We like to feel as though the product was created with us in mind. We feel a bit territorial about our favourite products, as though they were created for us alone. Think of your favourite cuddly toy from childhood. You would not have been happy to hear that several thousand other children had the exact same toy, because you thought of it as being yours alone. As adults we have products that we think of in the same way… a favourite pair of shoes, perhaps?

If a manufacturer changes the way they make a particular product, we may become quite upset. For example, a shoe brand changes the styling and fit of their running shoes. When you purchase your next pair of runners, you find them uncomfortable, develop blisters and are unable to wear them. You may feel quite exasperated as you exclaim, "I can't believe they changed my shoes!" The brand was seeking innovation, but lost a customer because they changed their product. The 'What' is personal and reliable.

Where: Customers are shopping online more than ever; therefore, it is necessary that the online shopping experience is a pleasant one. The service of shopping online is part of the brand experience. Many online retailers make it extraordinarily easy to purchase on their websites. The ease and convenience will keep customers returning frequently.

We've mentioned Amazon as a brand that makes online shopping convenient; another is John Lewis. They've responded to their customers' need for flexible options and convenience superbly. In addition to offering flexible delivery options to customers' homes, they also offer free delivery to John Lewis and Waitrose stores, selected by the customer in line with their own requirements and convenience.

This is a fantastic example of 'click & collect'. The customer orders online from anywhere (increasingly on mobiles and tablets) and then collects from the most convenient location for them, avoiding the frustration of not being at home when the delivery arrives! I understand over 50% of John Lewis' online sales over Christmas 2014 were click & collect. This is a significant change in shopping behaviour. Customers obviously love the convenience of shopping where they want, when they want and arranging delivery and 'collect' options to best suit their needs.

Shipping and delivery of online purchases are an important aspect of online shopping that is also a part of the brand experience, regardless of whether it is carried out by a third party. As I write, 44% of online shoppers abandon their shopping baskets because they are not happy with the delivery or shipping instructions. Brands need to pay attention to all aspects of the online shopping experience. The 'Where' is quick and easy.

It is paramount that you are tuned in to what your customers are saying about you. Your customer is your new CEO. To understand your customer, you have to walk in their shoes and learn their mind-set. The old, garden-fence style of communicating on a small scale has been replaced by numerous information-gathering sources. Communication has moved on; therefore, you have to be honest and open in your interactions with your customers. You must engage them and develop a relationship with them so that you will better understand them and serve them exceptionally.

Mojo Motion: The love your customers have for your product encompasses the connection and the experience they have over the transaction. Make sure it is a good experience! And, never forget to think like your customer.

Chapter 6
Colleagues Who Care

Your colleagues are the most important business assets you have! This is especially true in any customer-facing business where products and services are developed, communicated, sold, and delivered by people who effectively are the living representation of the brand. Success comes when your vision carries your entire team with you, not only your customers but your internal team as well. Your colleagues are the face of the brand! In chapter 5 we explored what it takes for a customer to love you and in chapter 6 we now need to take this a step further to explore what makes a business a great place to work.

What do your employees or business associates do to enhance your brand? Your colleagues are often the first human interaction people have with your brand, from the person answering the phone to the person greeting prospective customers at the door. They have an extraordinarily important role in what your customers take away from their experience in your store or business. You want your colleagues to love your brand as much as you do; they must embrace your mojo so they can share it with others. When your colleagues fall in love with your brand, they will genuinely convey this to your customers.

An employee who simply goes through the motions of processing the transaction will not leave much of an impression on your customer. An employee who answers the phone in a bored tone does not convey the thriving, energetic atmosphere of your brand. On the flipside, an employee who engages and builds rapport over the transaction, whether in person, over the phone, or online chat, will leave a lasting impression on your customers. The event will have morphed from a business transaction to an engaging interaction that will leave the customer wishing to return again and again. Your customers will fall in love with your brand and they may even fall in love with your engaging colleagues!

Think of a time you went shopping and encountered a wonderful representative. You may have purchased more than you had intended because you were enjoying the rapport with the salesperson. An effective, committed colleague will befriend a potential customer, establish camaraderie, and let the customer know that they are important to your brand, just as your brand is important to the customer.

When your brand values and beliefs come from within the company and are acutely understood and represented by your colleagues, they represent a motivated and inspired team on behalf of your brand. If your people are 'living the brand' in all that they do to deliver your product or service—the 'what', they will persuade your customers with ease.

The values your business embodies also need to be understood and believed by the people working in the business. If colleagues feel valued and recognised, they will be committed and happy. As a result, they will ensure that the customer benefits from a great experience. When your colleagues say 'I'm excited to come to work' or 'this is what we've been waiting for' or 'this makes me proud of what I do' you know you are onto something, that the passion for business and brand is alive and kicking afresh – that is the mojo!

So, what do you do to make your colleagues care about your brand? An employee who sees your brand through the brand lens and has experienced your brand first-hand will intuitively share the vision of your brand with your customers. This may sound simple, but often a brand owner may assume their employees already know the brand; it is worthwhile to take the time to share your brand vision and philosophy with each and every colleague who interacts with your customers.

Once you have shared your vision, your colleagues are much more likely to be able to think like your customers; this then becomes a virtuous circle. Discovering the brand essence will make your business, product, or service an integral part of the lives of your colleagues, just as it is for your customers. Essentially, to deliver a great customer experience, a business needs everyone to understand and believe in the vision for the business.

American President John F Kennedy visited NASA's Launch Operations Center, which has since been renamed Kennedy Space Center, three times in 1962 and 1963. During one of those visits, it is said that he came across a man sweeping the floor of one of the warehouses and chatted with him about his job. President Kennedy asked the man, "What do you do around here?" The man replied, "I'm helping to put a man on the moon!" This story exemplifies what it is all about! Everyone in the organisation understanding the vision, believing in this and understanding the contribution that they can make towards achieving it.

All colleagues employed by the company should be aware and understand the business 'why', as well as the 'what' and the 'how'. Additionally, it makes all the difference if they can relate to customers as people and to put themselves in the customers' shoes. Effectively, they are mirrors of each other, representing a true set of people relationships, on the inside and the outside of the business.

When colleagues authentically engage with customers, they will be an incredibly valuable asset to your company. The colleagues who are on the front lines of customer relations gain valuable insight from the customers that they can then pass on to you. Colleagues who know their input is valued will become skilled observers who attend to minute details. An attentive colleague will pay attention when a customer expresses their desires relating to your products and will pass this knowledge on to you.

In these days of social media there are no real dividing lines, just effective or less effective communication. It makes a huge difference if people at all levels and across different roles and functions in the company continue to communicate exceptionally well. If the business is to remain current with its finger on the pulse of customer desire, the senior team, board members, and business owners must remain fully connected with their customers and their colleagues. When there is true listening, rapport, and insight, as a consequence, the experience on the inside of the business will be fully congruent with the experience the customer receives.

There is no hiding place these days and if your brand's values are not being consistently embodied, it will be apparent to colleagues and customers. The experience the colleague has within their work environment is often very publicly shared. In addition to the more long-standing, traditional measures of employee experience, there are now websites where people publicly share their work experiences, for better — or worse. Obviously, you want your employees to sing the praises of your company and your brand! The genuine way to ensure your employees feel this way is to share your vision with them and make them a real, valued part of your team.

You and your brand stand for something compelling. Your brand essence, your mojo, the reason your brand exists at its most fundamental level, is to improve lives. When your colleagues share the goal of touching people and improving their lives, they will be inspired and united by the core beliefs of your brand. Motivational speaker Andy Harrington said, "If you aren't making enough money, you are simply not helping enough people." This is certainly an interesting way to look at it, isn't it? Improving the lives of your customers will help your customers get the results they want and you will get the result you want. It is truly amazing to watch colleagues embrace and believe in the brand they represent; and when they feel valued by the brand, they effortlessly make the customer feel valued in turn.

Make your brand essence compelling; articulate it brilliantly so that it stands out. Where unity is happening, colleagues will feel able to make the right decision to ensure the customer feels happy with the product, service, and experience they receive. They will act under their own initiative because they understand the principles the brand stands for and they will feel able and trusted to apply these appropriately.

In instances where colleagues do not comprehend the brand essence, something resembling a rulebook will be required. This will invariably remove the colleague's ability to relate on a personal level, which means the interactions with customers will become impersonal, as well.

Let me be more specific with a few examples that occurred over a day's shopping excursion. We began with breakfast at Bill's. This restaurant's values are "to serve really good food, to make sure every customer has a good time, and to go a bit further to make sure Bill's is always somewhere people want to come back to." Well, I can vouch for that! Our waiter went out of his way to make sure that each person at our table selected exactly what was right for them. There was no upselling or pressure; rather, we were served the right food for us. The service and attention were impeccable. Rather than a quick inquiry as to whether the food was to our liking, the waiter asked each of us questions tailored to our own experiences. Outstanding!

After breakfast, we went to Ted Baker to shop for a dress for my stepdaughter. She is a teenager who was dressed in shorts, t-shirt, and trainers. The experienced staff at Ted Baker helped us find the perfect dress and shoes for her. A casual, young girl walked into the dressing room, but a princess emerged from it! The metamorphosis was amazing! The sales staff were tuned in to their product and their customer; consequently, the results were nothing short of magical.

To contrast the experiences at Bill's and Ted Baker, let me tell you about our experience at a shoe store that day. On entry, it was immediately obvious that the store was understaffed. There were far more customers than sales staff on the floor. Additionally, the stock rooms were not well organised because the staff struggled to find items, causing a build-up of waiting, exasperated customers. As the stress levels escalated, the staff became more and more frustrated and overwhelmed, which they communicated to their customers.

Interestingly, this particular shoe store attempts to motivate their salespeople with money by paying a commission on each item sold. This is not usually a good way to motivate staff, and once things begin to get difficult it is definitely not going to work.

Yes, you want your sales staff to be concerned with making sales, but consider their motivation. If they are working on commission, they will dismiss an irritated customer knowing a fresh face will walk in shortly. If they are motivated to sell your product because they genuinely love the brand and want to deliver your brand essence to the customer, they will do everything within their power to ensure each customer receives it. When your colleagues are engaged with your story and your brand, they retain their composure and rapport with your customers when things are not going smoothly.

I had another frustrating shopping experience one day when I was attempting to return an article of clothing to a premium designer's area inside Harvey Nichols. The shirt had been worn only once and a seam was giving way. It was obvious that the shirt had a defect, so I knew I had a case for a fairly easy return.

The sales associate told me that she could not return my money. Instead, she said she would have to send the shirt to the head office to determine if it was actually faulty. I remained calm and tried to work with the associate to encourage her to think of me, the customer. She was clearly not comfortable making decisions of this kind and she was afraid of making the wrong decision and getting in trouble with her manager if she gave my money back.

I asked her to call for a Harvey Nichols manager in an attempt to move this situation along. The Harvey Nichols representative suggested to the sales associate that she re-think her decision not to refund my money. Unfortunately, the Harvey Nichols representative could not require the sales associate for the premium brand to process the return. Most people would have given up and left with a defective shirt, or they would've become angry and escalated the situation into a shouting match. I remained calm even though I was extremely disappointed that this particular store valued keeping my money in their till over my satisfaction with their product.

Your customers' satisfaction is paramount! A company that understands this and puts it into practice is Hanna Andersson. They value quality and comfort for their young clients. An American friend bought a Hanna Andersson sleeper for her toddler. After this sleeper had been worn for over eighteen months, the zip gave way. By this time, the sleeper was getting to be a bit short at the arms and legs, but it was still a beloved favourite. My friend contacted Hanna Andersson to let them know the zip broke. The sales associate apologised for the broken zip on the well-worn pyjamas and offered to send a new, replacement sleeper. While processing the transaction, the sales associate noticed the purchase had been made over two years ago and immediately up-sized the replacement sleeper! My friend tells me that she now only buys Hanna Andersson for baby shower gifts and tells all of her friends about the amazing quality of the clothing as well as the outstanding customer service. She has become a true ambassador!

Before an employer chooses to hire an employee, that person has already chosen to work for the business. In other words, your prospective employees have committed to you before you have met them or interviewed them. Engage with your colleagues so that they deliver your brand essence through a knockout customer experience day in, day out, and it will make your business, product, or service the first choice for your customer, every time.

Mojo Motion: Understand the vision and have pride in the brand and business. Articulate your brand essence well to your colleagues and make them a valued part of your team so that they love your brand as much as you do. They will naturally turn a business transaction into a fun, engaging event that keeps your customers coming back for more!

Chapter 7
Creating Your Own Love Affair

This book began with the story of my journey, so perhaps it is not surprising that my everyday behaviour (what starts within me and is shared with others) also has a strong sense of balance, plus a dose of 'need to crack on'. I believe that insight, energy, and empathy need to be hand in hand. I told you that I would open up and share more about myself as our relationship, dear reader, develops. I feel that we have come to a level of intimacy where I can share a bit more about myself.

I met David at age 16, married him at 23, and we divorced at 25. We were clearly too young to be married. I then met Mike while on a buying trip for Tesco. I married him at age 27 and we had two beautiful children together. We were very happily married for twenty years before his life was tragically cut short at the age of 47, when Emily was 16 and Lewis 13. Our lives were changed forever; it took many years for us all to find a new normal and really learn to enjoy life again.

I met David again about six years ago, having kept in close touch with his mother and brother. We began a new romantic relationship. Our bond has deepened over time and we were married in July 2015, in the company of all four of our children, Emily, Lewis, Antonia and Hugo, as well as my 91-year-old father, my sister and her family. We followed up the ceremony with a fabulous party for over eighty friends and family from all over the world!

I realise these recent developments sound like a romantic fairy-tale. Things have not exactly been so rosy, though. One year after Mike died, David's mother passed away. Six months later his brother committed suicide, leaving him the only remaining member of his nuclear family. When we reconnected, a new bond was formed between us out of the adversities we'd both faced. David and I have truly become partners, romantically and domestically, in life's journey.

Our stepchildren have bonded with each of us and with each other. David's children enjoy spending time with me and he has really taken Lewis under his wing. Lewis had a bit of a rough time after losing his father. He chose not to attend college and had no real direction in life when David stepped in and offered him the opportunity to spend time in Cape Town and to help in one of his businesses. As my youngest, Lewis is now thrilled to have a younger brother. David and I are more adult friends than stepparents to each other's children.

The life experiences I have shared over the course of our developing relationship have taught me to be very insightful. I see this insight as the 'head' part of my everyday behaviour. I am quick to grasp the situation and understand what needs to be done, and the best way forward is rooted in intuition. My intuition is based on understanding and analysing the broad context of a given situation.

It is, however, my empathetic nature that creates my 'tone of voice'. This is the 'heart' of my everyday behaviour. I do not use my experience in an arrogant or 'shouty' way. Indeed the opposite is true. Empathy starts from wanting to listen, to being open to the other point of view. I feel genuine warmth and generosity towards the other party. I yearn to support them in what they are trying to achieve. I strive to do all of this in a way that can inspire, energise, and lead to a new way of looking at the situation.

My desire is to feed my roots and live my passion of insight and empathy to help a company, team, or indeed my own family to 'crack on'. When people 're-discover the mojo' or, on occasion, 'discover the mojo' after working with me, it means that the experience they've had led them to a renewed sense of purpose, values, and beliefs. This experience is one that re-energises and excites the spirit, the swagger, the confidence and passion of the company or the project and those involved.

In the process of creating The Brand Inspiration co., I have been extremely fortunate to work with colleagues, bosses, and peers who have guided, encouraged and inspired me. As a result of these interactions and experiences, I've honed my proven approach to give a renewed sense of purpose, values, and beliefs to businesses. I work with my clients to re-energise them, excite the spirit, the swagger and the confidence in their business to really connect with their customers. This relationship creates the difference between winning and losing in the marketplace. I love to help businesses achieve success through discovering (or rediscovering) the mojo of the business or brand, for an exciting future.

My approach is based on an apparently simple concept that I have already shared with you —the 'why', the 'what' and the 'how'. I have found that my approach can reliably persuade the hearts and minds of businesses, stakeholders, boards, colleagues, and customers to unite in their passion for and belief in the brand, with compelling results.

I certainly have not followed a career plan; rather I have been open-minded to opportunities as they have arisen and I've followed my instincts about what felt right at each stage when faced with a choice to make. I've always been guided by my principles; I need to feel that I am able to add real value, work with people I respect and trust, and feel a sense of fulfilment with whatever I am doing.

In addition to my closest colleagues and leaders, I've worked with wonderful people in my network of contacts, friends, agencies and collaborators. Each of these are outstanding people who have stimulated my thinking and challenged me when I've needed it. Whether you are just starting out with a brilliant business idea or you are a well-established brand needing a profitable makeover, I trust you have discovered that my approach can work for you.

At The Brand Inspiration co., I draw on my extensive network of specialist collaborators to ensure you get the range of expertise you need, which will deliver the results you want. This is not a one-size-fits-all methodology! Rather, the 'why', the 'what' and the 'how' combine to create a highly flexible approach that can work for you whatever stage you are at in the life of your business or brand. I have a passion for (re)discovering the mojo, which could mean unprecedented success for you!

I have motivated and inspired whole business teams in top companies to achieve belief-driven action. I have mentored and coached individuals, entrepreneurs, and small businesses on the path to greatness. I have led the transformation of highly commercial brands to achieve qualitative and quantitative shifts in business performance. And we have had a lot of fun along the way!

At Harvey Nichols, initially as a seventeen-year-old Management Trainee, I was surrounded by many inspiring, glamorous, efficient women. These mentors were there to guide me in a whole variety of 'dos and don'ts' including, for example, the protocol of serving members of The Royal Family on occasions. My senior Harvey Nichols colleagues shaped me and offered so much to aspire to, continuing to offer support when I achieved my first fully-fledged appointment as Childrenswear Buyer at the grand old age of 23!

The buying office at Tesco presented a very different set of learning experiences, as I learned about the cost of raw materials and met a far wider group of customers than I'd been exposed to in Knightsbridge.

Over twenty-three years ago, I was just back from maternity leave and working as the BHS client representative with the McKinsey team while they sought to understand the BHS customer and what 'real choice' represented to them. This is where I began to understand the potential of truly listening to your customer and translating the insights gained into a compelling customer experience.

It was quite a surprise when talking to BHS customers to learn that more 'real choice' could actually mean fewer products. And then to witness fewer products turn into a 20% increase in sales for BHS was a wonderful experience. It was the moment it hit me that, in this case, the 'why' for the customer was way more important than the actual product, the 'what'.

When introducing a somewhat radical idea, success means carrying everyone with you; not only the customer, but the internal team, also. On this project, my own experience as a buyer meant I could empathise with the buyers, speak their language, and gain their trust. Perhaps a little wary in the beginning, they began to turn to me for advice and guidance. This was a sure sign of their belief in the fresh approach I was proposing.

I am able to connect with the business team and encourage them to get behind a new approach. For example, I connected the Wallis woman with the existing 'pattern room upstairs' which brought everyone on board with the new approach. I was appointed the first ever Marketing Director for Wallis and was delighted to be working for a business with many talented and passionate people, although I knew they were a bit unsure of what to expect from me. I knew I needed to build trust.

I particularly respected the design team at Wallis, some of whom had trained with a number of the most iconic names in the design world. But we learned through research that the potential Wallis customer was someone who was seeking 'distinctive design they could enjoy' and had no idea of the strong design credentials behind the clothes they could be wearing. The Dress to Kill campaign boldly connected the Wallis woman with the sharpness and flair of the existing 'pattern room upstairs', and Wallis at last stood out from a 'me, too' high street, for qualities, values, and beliefs it already had. This ad campaign is still used as a case study in Media Degree courses as an example of a stand-out campaign on a moderate budget. I am honoured to have been a part of it. I loved the Wallis brand and enjoyed my experience there hugely.

The moment when I realise you have the 'why' just waiting there to transform everything makes the hair on the back of my neck stand up! I hope these examples demonstrate how I can help you streamline your 'why'.

Now let's talk 'how'. This is an example of how I used the customer's viewpoint, in this case a kid's eye view, to affect the 'why' and the 'how'. My children were seven and four when I was lured to Early Learning Centre (ELC), so I was tuned in to a child's viewpoint. This was an unforgettable and altogether different experience.

We listened to the customers, both the children and their parents. ELC was a trusted brand, but not that much fun as it was a bit more library than play store. This was a challenging time as ELC was losing money. We set about 'enriching the lives of children'. We took the toys out of the boxes in our stores and our customer-facing teams chose to wear T-shirts and trousers so they could get down on their hands and knees to play with their customers. We literally took a kid's-eye view and, in what may have seemed a slightly risky move, even closed the stores to sales one morning a week so the pressure to buy was alleviated and the kids could simply have fun trying out the toys for real.

Parents told us how great it was to know what to buy with confidence, having seen first-hand what their children loved to play with. Other customers told us they could hear the laughter when they opened the pages of our new catalogues. The energy, resilience and determination required to be part of what it took to turn a business round from a £7m loss to a £10m profit was something I'd not experienced before (or since). This turnaround took place because we delivered an extraordinary and consistent customer experience!

I can only describe my four years at Ann Summers as 'priceless'. There cannot be another business like it. It was a wonderful opportunity to help a brand rediscover its mojo. I led a team to articulate the brand essence of 'fearlessly unleashing sexual confidence', aligning it with values expressed by the business teams involved. This gave the business renewed confidence and provided the inspiration for all key strategic decisions, including product, communication, and overall direction towards the vision.

Even the media feedback regarding Ann Summers became increasingly positive, with publicity turning strong for the brand. I am often asked, "Now, what was it really like?" Well, I can tell you that all the normal retail conversations took place, but it is never quite the same when the product under discussion is a sex toy of some kind rather than something more mundane. There was never a dull moment!

More recently, I have been working with the small business sector, as well as with startups. I have so much empathy for small business owners and entrepreneurs! I am proud to have recently been invited by the Chair and Founder, Karen Richards, to be Deputy Chair and Director of Women in Retail. This is a members' community established to nurture the connections and talent of accomplished women in retail; we will soon be welcoming emerging leaders into our community enabling a wider group of women to share the benefits of the support and personal and professional development. I am thoroughly enjoying this very real opportunity to give something back to the industry that has enabled, motivated, and inspired me to take my experience and expertise out to a wider marketplace with the launch of The Brand Inspiration co. in 2014. My vision is to help businesses and brands '(re)discover their mojo'.

Women in Retail is a great example of 'mojo-finding' at its best. Founded by Karen Richards ten years ago, Women in Retail is a not-for-profit organisation. Karen set up an informal community in response to demand from a group of peers who were united in the need for a forum to connect with like-minded women in the sector. The group evolved into a more established organisation from 2005 and has developed into the fantastic community we all enjoy today, that is about to embark on the next stage of its exciting journey.

Karen and I first met in 2007 when I became involved with Women in Retail as a member and we became firm friends. As our friendship has deepened, we have collaborated and supported each other in numerous ways in both a work and personal context.

Karen's achievement in establishing this wonderful community almost single handedly until she invited a group of Trustees to support her is amazing and she's done this alongside a full time job, motherhood and a long distance commute!

Women in Retail has established itself as the community for accomplished women in the sector to connect, meet and share experiences. Our values are courage, confidence, collaboration, warmth, energy, fun, trust, and shared experience. The work that Karen and I are doing together is ensuring a fantastic future for Women in Retail.

Our purpose is to create an environment where increasing numbers of women are recognised for their contribution in senior leadership roles. We engage with other women and mentor them as they encounter challenges in the retail industry. All senior members are encouraged to offer advice, counsel, and support to other members. We create connections, enable friendships, stimulate ideas, develop thought leadership, enhance personal and professional development, offer support, and nurture emerging leaders. This builds confidence, which leads to improved performance.

A quote from a member, CEO of a Multi Channel Fashion Brand: "I protect my Women in Retail event time in my diary at almost all costs and I know I'm not alone. I find the events invaluable and so enjoyable, too." It is a wonderful organisation and I have been proud to help them find their mojo!

Another brand, led by a strong businesswoman, which I have been excited to work with is Isossy Children. This is a relatively young brand that offers fashion with a global culture for children. Amanda Rabor is the woman behind this brand; her vision is to 'inspire the confidence, creativity and self-belief of children growing up and living in diverse, global cultures'. About five years into the business, Amanda was feeling a bit jaded and unsure of how to proceed. I am thrilled that she called me and we were able to work out a Mojo-discovering plan for her business.

Using insight and empathy, I was able to ascertain deeper aspects of her vision by exploring Amanda's motivations and journey with Isossy Children. We adjusted the 'handwriting' of her business and set a new tone for moving forward. We developed clear outcomes and objectives, along with putting a timeline in place. Regarding working with me, Amanda said, "It's an all-encompassing experience which ultimately empowered and focused my business vision."

I have also enjoyed working with Amanda's sister, Denise Rabor of Leadership 3Sixty. This company has a passion for development and leadership. They aim to educate, motivate, inspire and challenge. They desire to share 'their point of view along with your experiences.' I am thrilled to have been 'In Conversation With' Leadership 3Sixty. Not content with just one business, Denise also runs WOW Beauty, a wonderful accessible 'go to' brand for beauty advice.

Whatever the nature of the transformation required, I know that I and my network of expert collaborators have the potential to add significant value to your business. I enjoy working with all businesses and people with and for whom I can make a difference and help them get from where they are to where they need to be. I offer a range of approaches to achieving this, depending on the people involved and the needs of the business. I offer my services via consultancy, where I carry out a piece of work on behalf of the client. Alternatively, I offer business growth coaching and/or mentoring to facilitate the brand owner doing the work themselves.

TSM Meridian was established in 2011 and I was able to come on board and help them find their Mojo. Elizabeth Gordon, the Assistant Director, says, "Fiona has been an invaluable asset to our business; she has an incredible skill in transforming concepts into tangible actions; she is extremely bright, a pleasure to work with, and had has an infectious positive energy. By working with Fiona we have made huge progress, articulated our brand and been highly motivated to set and achieve exciting goals. She is very committed and has made many helpful and interesting introductions to her impressive network of connections. I cannot imagine not having Fiona as a presence in our business, and would strongly recommend her to any business or entrepreneur needing support in realising their ambitions and potential." These are very kind words and I am thrilled to have been a part of helping TSM Meridian discover its mojo.

TSM Meridian has created a stunning brand and a unique product that launches summer 2015. The brand is LUVSENSE london, they create seductive accessories to enhance intimacy and indulge the senses. Their first product to market is the LUVVU mirror, a beautifully designed, sleek and stylish mirror that can be easily attached to a ceiling for enjoyment and discreetly stored when not in use. The launch of the LUVVU mirror follows 5 years of extensive market research and product development and fulfils a unique position in the adult playtime market.

Certainly, I will dig deep to discover the brand essence that connects you with your customers and that will make your business, product or service an integral and irreplaceable part of their lives. I will personally talk to you, your teams, your customers and your stakeholders and ask the questions that get to the heart of your brand. I am known for my ability to discover the emotional and rational hooks that will make your brand irresistible and compelling. I will work together with you to clearly articulate your brand so that you, your whole organisation and your customers will be captivated.

I will not create a brand concept as separate add-on to your business, as many traditional brand strategy agencies do. I will seek the heart of your brand in your strengths, in who you are and what you do best, in what you already stand for, or want to stand for. Together, you and I will breathe life into every strand of your organisation, carrying your whole team with you, with impressive results.

I believe that the brand is the business and the business is the brand; for success, the two must be one and the same. The product, its price, your colleagues, your service, the selling environment, that bit of extra-special something you might never have thought of or dared to try on your own. I will ensure that every aspect of the customer journey is considered, so that you deliver a seamless and winning customer experience—wherever and whenever your multi-channel customer chooses to engage or shop with you. Then you can deliver on the brand promise and delight your customers, day in, day out.

Brand and business must be one and the same for long-term success, so I will give you tools to evaluate your whole organisation in line with your brand essence. I will show you how to measure the progress of your brand and guide you to keep it fresh and relevant to your customers in a fast-changing world. You will become brave yet disciplined as you begin to look outward rather than inward. You will instinctively and constantly put yourselves into the shoes of your customers to stay innovative for them and connected to them. Your business or brand will absolutely have discovered or rediscovered its mojo, and you'll be feeling confident in the strength of your brand and excited for its future!

Having helped you develop a clear articulation of your brand, vision and values, I will work with you to ensure the strength of your product handwriting and customer proposition. From here you will be ready to develop a road map to grow your business through the relevant growth strategy, including a sales and marketing strategy to support your requirements. I will help you decide the best choice of consultancy coaching and mentoring to meet your needs.

Are you ready to (re)discover the mojo yet?

Epilogue
A Long-Term Affair

"Today is the slowest day of change for the rest of our lives"
- Martjn Bertisen, Director Retail, Google UK.

Indeed, the world is changing rapidly! The most successful businesses are those that manage to think like a customer and embrace this rapid pace of change. These businesses, both large and small, are always innovating and evolving, while remaining true to their brand and the customer proposition.

There are numerous, small, nimble, entrepreneurial businesses that are leaping in and disrupting the market as they do not feel the difficulties and barriers that the more established players often struggle to overcome. As friend and colleague, Sophie Albizua from Enova, recently said, "If you see an opportunity, go after it or be ready for a 15 year-old budding entrepreneur to get there first!" So true, don't you think?

I love working with smaller businesses; my approach with them tends to be business growth coaching and mentoring. It is all about helping the business owner do it themselves. I am currently working with Earthmonk, a very young, exciting company, and cannot wait to see what will happen!

In addition to working with large businesses, small businesses, and startups, I am also a member of several organisations where I provide mentoring services. One of these is the Westminster Business Council. I was approached and asked to become a mentor with their programme because of my track record helping businesses find their mojo. I am thrilled to be able to offer my guidance and support to the businesses within the Westminster Business Council.

In addition to working with the Westminster Business Council, I am also a Registered Business Growth Service Expert, delivering support on behalf of the Business Growth Service. The Business Growth Service, that now incorporates Growth Accelerator and the Manufacturing Advisory Service, is a government backed service offering support to businesses with the potential to improve and grow. The aim of the Business Growth Service is to help businesses achieve their growth potential through the provision of tailored support. I thoroughly enjoy coaching business owners as they strive to reach their full potential.

Additionally, I am a member of The Chambers. This is a private network of independent consultants sharing a passion to bring innovation to organisations. The Chambers believes in collaborative thinking, we have a strong track record of success across a broad range of industries and disciplines. Our motto is 'We evolve, we network, we collaborate.'

Another organisation I belong to is BNI. This is the world's largest referral and professional networking organisation, whose purpose is to help members grow their businesses. BNI is geared towards creating relationships to further your business.

This isn't the whole story, so you'll need to come back for more. Although this is the end of the book, let's not let it be the end of our affair. There are so many things happening at the moment. Check my website to discover what I'm working on now: www.thebrandinspirationco.com.

Stop by and (re)discover the mojo!